By
Raymond Florio

First print 2007

For distribution
raymondflorio@yahoo.com

<u>Cover Credits</u>
Cover Design: Richard Lewis rlewis63@kc.rr.com
Cover Concept: Raymond Florio

Printed in the United States of America

First and foremost I would like to thank God for giving me the gift and allowing me to share the gift with others. Next I would like to thank the 3 J's..... Julius, Jasmine and Jamari my three wonderful children. (Daddy loves you!!) And last but certainly not least, I would like to thank you the reader for supporting me. Please understand that I am a plant so expose me to all your warm love, and watch me blossom and grow.

-Raymond Florio

*This book is a compilation of **"Poems and Proverbs"** (wise sayings) which I have written throughout the years. One poem **"Old Drunk Joe"** dates all the way back to 1982. It was the very first poem I ever wrote. I've tried to include **"Poems and Proverbs"** (wise sayings) which address many of the social issues that we face today. So from 1982 all the way to 2006 you will read and feel what a labor of love this, my first project has been.*

Remember slow and steady wins the race. There is a writer in all of us. So grab a pen.

A Man So Small

I used to think
I had the answers to it all,
But now I realize
I was a man so small.

I used to think
My ego made me so tall,
But now I realize
I was a man so small.

I used to think
I could fly so high
And never fall,
But now I realize
I was a man so small.

I used to think
I could do it all
With no help,
But now I realize
I was a man so small,
'Cause it was you
Who held my hand
As I took my very
first step.

"Dear John"

I know the good book says *"thou shalt not kill"*,

But you're gone and it doesn't even seem real.

One senseless act has left a tremendous hole to

Be filled and for the one who took your life, even

If we took his, it's a no win cause you would still

Be missed by your family and kids. Dear John,

Memories of you running through my mind, it's

Such a shame you're just another victim of black,

On black crime.

This Poem is dedicated to
John Roosevelt McCleod McCullough II

ဢၢၺဢၢၺဢၢၺဢၢၺဢၢၺ

Words

Magical, mystical and mysterious

Merely mumbo jumbo when loosely fitted

But add rhyme to the rhythm and words become

serious.

＄ＯＣ＆＄ＯＣ＆＄ＯＣ＆＄ＯＣ＆＄ＯＣ＆

Sex

Hot,

Raw *and*

Steamy.

Cool,

Sticky *and*

Creamy.

Man

Civilized
But yet untamed.

Knowledge
But yet no brain.

Animal instincts deep within.

Self taught righteousness,
Provoking sin.

This is how
I know man to be.

Look in the mirror,
And you'll see ME.

I Cried

I cried after the first time
I held your hand,
'Cause I knew
That I would tattoo
Your name across my heart,
And that together,
We would create
A brand new start,
And that life's problems
Wouldn't seem so bad,
'Cause I had you
As my support,
My staff, my better half,
My morning breath,
In sickness and in health,
In life till death.

Kenya

Your name screams
Mother Africa,
The birth place of us all.

Your beauty rivals
That of ancient queens,
Where men rush
To answer your every
Beck and call.

But what good is a queen
Without a king?

It only means
She has no one
To share her dreams.

Nobody's Fool

I'm only the Fool,
'Cause I choose to be,

Not the Fool
'Cause I have to be.

So who's really the Fool?
You or Me?

Let There Be Light

Let there be light
To guide me through
Each new day,
And when I am lost,
Let there be light
To help me find my way.

And at times
When I am selfish,
Let there be light
To help me give.

Let there be light
Each day that I live.

Friends

Friends are like
The seasons;

They come and they go.

But you'll never be lonely
If **God** is the one person
That you know.

Old Drunk Joe

Old Drunk Joe,
When sober,
Was a good man to know.

But I would
Sit on his lap,
And the lies would begin
As he nursed his
Bottle of gin.

Have Faith

Have faith in yourself
And in the things
That you believe,

'Cause a little faith
Is all that you need
To make the things
That you dream for
Come true.

'Cause with a little faith,
It will all come to you.

Have faith.

The Meaning of life

What is the meaning
Of life?

The answer is simple.

You'll know that your life
Has been worth while
If you're able to look back
And smile.

That is the true meaning
Of life.

Rich Man Poor Man

A poor man
Once asked a rich man,
"Do you control money;
Or does money control you?"

The rich man, unable
To reply,
Simply looked at the
Poor man with
A bewildered look
In his eyes.

Black in America

Being Black in America
Means I'm scaring ya,
Daring ya to include
Me in the dreams
That's meant for all Americans,
Not just the ones
Born with the silver spoons
Or the ones granted access
Soon as they pass through
The womb.
What about the dreams
Of my ancestors,
Who lie buried
In their tombs?
It's our responsibility
To ourselves and to society
To be like the marines –
The best that we can be.
But how can that be
When we don't even
Get out and V-O-T-E?
I wonder does it even
Matter that much
To the current generation
That our time here
On earth meant nothing
As we return to dust.

CRCRCRCRCR

Sad-Faced Clown

They say the world's
A stage for a clown,

When the show is over
and the final curtain comes down,
who really cries for a clown?

Cause under the white painted face
and bright red nose
lies a tortured soul.

The Sin I'm In

The Sin I'm In
Is the color black.

It's the fact
That gives them
The right to attack.

Something Missing

When I woke up
This morning,
The sun was shining bright,
But something was missing.
It just didn't feel right.

All day at work,
I couldn't concentrate

Question: Could it have been
Something that I ate?

So as I sat at my desk
And tried to reminiscence,

I remembered what I
Had missed.

It was as simple
As this:

A sweet kiss
From your tasty lips.

ಶಿಂದಿಂದಿಂದಿಂದಿ

Coco Dream

Sweet,

Seductive,

Sexy,

Sultry,

Succulent,

Satisfying.

Smile

It's not an apple,
But a smile a day
That keeps the
Doctor away,

'Cause every time you smile,
You let your inner child
Come out and play.

Nobody Knows

Nobody Knows
The contents of a man's soul,

Whether it's solid gold
Or a lump of coal.

By God,
That's a story to be told,

'Cause in His hands,
The balance He holds.

Game Called Life

We all know
That this game called life
Can sometimes
Cut like a knife,

Whether it's wrong
Or whether it's right.

But you can't give up the fight,
And the poor don't
Always get their share.

But then again,
Whoever said that life
Was fair?

L-O-V-E

L-O-V-E
Can set you free.
It can end
The world's pain and misery.

Spread a little L-O-V-E
And see if it doesn't help.

Remember you were told
To L-O-V-E your neighbor
As thyself.

I Hunger for You

Whether it's Breakfast,
Lunch
Or dinner,

Baby, my hunger for you
Makes me a sinner.

Hot, raw, uncut lust.
I want you so bad,
I'm about to bust.

Thoughts of you
Keep running through my mind.

I'm reminiscing about
The last freaky time
We took the number sixty-nine
And made it shine.

I don't know
What I'm gonna do,
'Cause, girl, I hunger for you.

What Else Can I Do?

When you say I'm wrong,
I'm wrong.

When you say get lost,
I'm gone.

When you say come home,
I come home.

Questions:
Am I a puppy dog
Or am I full grown?

Monogamy

Player till the day I die.

It was more than a statement.
It was more like a battle cry.

Why have one
When you can have plenty?

To make a dollar,
It takes a hundred pennies.

But when you have one –
The right one
Who makes your heart
Hotter than the sun,
That's when you know
Your night is complete
And your search is done.

Till the End of Time

I wish I could add
Some more time
To the end of time,
So you can realize
How long you'll always,
Forever be mine.

Maybe I should say
Two lifetimes or two lifelines.

But that still wouldn't justify
The love of mine –

How we'll always be intertwined
Body, Soul and Mind
Till the end of time.

Think of Me

Think of me
When there's no light.
Think of me
When you're done at night.
Think of me
When all your dreams
Seem so far out of sight.
Think of me
When you're ready to quit
The fight.
Think of me
When you shiver with fright.
Remember the nights
That I held you tight.
Think of me
When you ask yourself,
Is this wrong
Or is this right?
Think of me,
And I'm sure
That you'll see the light.
When you're locked in chains,
Think of me,
And you'll be free.
When in doubt, think
Of me.

I Used To Love Her

I used to love her,
But that was a long
Time ago.
Now she's loving another
Brother,
And I just can't let go.
Oh, I think back
To the times
When she used to be mine –
How our lips and hips
Used to be locked and intertwined.
My brother, please believe me;
This girl was so damn fine,
I was definitely
Under her spell.
I used to ask myself,
Could this be heaven
Or could this be hell?
Yeah, I was her puppy-dog fool, breaking all
The rules.
I was ready to play Mr. Mom.
Forget being a player.
Forget being cool.
And even though
She's loving another brother,
For me, they'll never
Be another.
Ain't no doubt about it.
Yeah, I used to love her.

My Voice

My voice shall be heard
Higher than any place
That an eagle can soar.

My voice will be louder
Than the mightiest lions roar.

My voice will collapse buildings
And move mountains.

My voice will remain pure
Like water flowing from
A river's fountain.

My voice will be the voice
Of those with little hope
Or no choice.

My voice will be the voice
Of those who came to
This country in little
Freedom boats.

My voice
Will offer clear, precise insight.

My voice
Will be the fuel
That's used to ignite the fight.

My voice
Will be the one
That rings out
In the middle of the night.

My voice
Will be the one
That replaces the wrong
With the right.

And with my voice,
I will scream till I'm hoarse.

'Cause I will use my voice
Till I lose my voice.

It's my choice.

It's my voice.

The Rage in Me

The rage in me
Keeps the fire a glow.

All I can think about is yes when I'm told no.

No steel doors
Or prison bars for me.

I want to be
Like the bird – totally free
With nothing but the sky
As my limit.

I can't stop – won't stop
Till I climb that highest mountain top.

With the need to succeed,
The rage in me
Forces me to achieve
The impossible dream.

Questions and Answers

If I said
I was sorry a thousand times,
Would it be enough for you
To forgive me and once
Again share your love?

If I climbed the
Highest mountain,
Would that prove to you
That I wanted to burn
In your eternal flame?

If I walked to hell
And back
With just one shoe,
Tell me,
Would that mean anything
To you?

If I said twenty-four
Hours wasn't enough time
To have you on my mind,
So I filmed a clock
And pressed rewind instead
So I could have forty-eight
Hours of you running
Through my head –

33

If I said there
Was no tea sweeter
Than the kisses
That you give to me,
Tell me, would you believe me?

If I promised to cry tears
Of joy every night
For the rest of my life –
If you would give me
The honor of being my wife,
Could we start tonight?

7-Day Love Affair

Day One:
I was nervous, so I lied
About an accident
To get to know your name.

Day Two:
I kept staring at the clock,
Trying to remember the clothes
You wore
And the way you walked.

Day Three:
I was bored sitting at home
Alone, looking at the *JET*
Beauty of the week.
Then I decided to call you,
'Cause I said to myself,
I know someone just
As sweet.

Day Four:
We agreed to meet for drinks.
I was just sitting at the
Table, drinking my drink
And counting my blessings,
'Cause you were wearing
A dress that could
have gotten you arrested.

Days Five and Six:
Were slow to come,
But I remember day seven,
'Cause that was the night
When the two of us
Became one,
And we laughed
At the morning sun.

If It Wasn't for the Money

If it wasn't for the money,
Maybe we could stop being
Brain-dead, political monkeys.

And if it wasn't for the money,
Maybe we could be real
With each other
Instead of being so phony.

And if it wasn't for the money,
Maybe we could spend more time
With our children
Instead of being slaves
To the system.

Yeah, if it wasn't
For the money.

It Hurts Me

It hurts me
When I see
Young brothers and sisters
Not using the wisdom
That was given
And ending up being trapped
In the system.

And it hurts me
When I see
Young brothers and sisters
Who never listen
No matter what.

Full of life and energy,
They never
Reach their potential.

They just self destruct.

Tell Me Your Name

Hey, pretty lady,
I wanna know your name.

I wanna be the moth
That burns in your flame.

If given the time,
I know that I could
Captivate your mind.

We could walk and hold hands.
You could be my woman.
I could be your man.

We could talk
About our future and
What tomorrow might hold.

We could tell our
Grandkids
How we met
When we get old.

Or you could
Tell me your name,
And I could simply walk away
And maybe fall in love
Some other day.

Face of God

As I look in the mirror,
It becomes a little clearer;
I see the face of God,
Not just another nigger
With roots to Adam
All the way back to Africa –
Much more than a slave
Born to be a master.

Jesus was the example,
For I am the face of God,
One of God's true angels.

People in the 80's

People losing their minds.

People lost in time.

People going nowhere fast.

People living in the past.

People on the brink.

People on the edge.

People sleeping in the streets,
'Cause they got no beds.

People got no homes.

People out of work.

They work all their lives.
They never have meat.
They just have bones.

Champion

In every day
And every dawn,
There's a man
Who must carry the
Legend on –

A man who rises
Above the rest,
A man who strives
To be the best.

A man who has
Become accustomed to pain,
A man who laughs
In the face of defeat,
A man who knows
Victory to be bittersweet.

A man who always
Does the very best
That he can.

Believe me, I know,
For I am such a man.

My Soul Aches

My soul aches
Every time I turn
On the news,
And I see a little kid
Getting abused.

My soul aches
Every time I think about
Our public schools,
Turning out nothing
But illiterate fools.

My soul aches
Every time I see a politician
Lying to my face
And then kissing my ass
During the November race.

My soul aches
When I think of all
The self hate.

My soul aches
Every time I think about
How my race is
Continually being raped.
My soul aches.

Time

Time is constantly
Slipping away,
And before you know it,
You'll be old and gray.

So make the most
Of every day,
'Cause time is constantly
Slipping away.

Memories

Here's to the memories
Of today and of yesterday,
When loving each other
Was the only way.

You loving me
And me loving you,
Loving each other
Till we were both blue.

I shall never forget
The time we spent together.
Fear not; though we
Are apart,
I shall love you forever.

Have Mercy

Have Mercy on me,
For I have suffered
So long,
And I've taken
All that I can take.

Even a heart that's strong
Can break.

I'm only human,
So I'm allowed
To make a few mistakes.

So I beg of thee,
Please have mercy on me.

Am I God

As I look in the mirror
At my facial features,
I stare very hard
And ask myself this question:
Am I God?

Do I have the power
To make a difference
In people's lives?
Am I the all-knowing
One; is that the reason
Why I can give advice?
Or am I just being selfish,
Trying to live my life twice?

I would like to be God
To be able to make
A difference
In people's lives,
Erase the pain
And correct the wrong
With the right,
And expose those
Who are blind to the light.
Yeah, I would like
To think that I was God.

What Would You Change?

What would you change
If you could change?
Would you change
The inner workings of a man's brain?

Would you change his heart
So that he could feel your pain?

Would you change places
And walk a mile in his shoes
So you could see the world
From his point of view?

What would you change?
Would you change
The current political system
To make us all equal instead
Of all victims?

Would you prevent hurricane Katrina?
Would you play God
And turn the hands back
On the clock?
Would you prevent Iraq?

What would you change
If you could change?

Would you prevent
AIDS, sickness and disease?

Would you put a chicken
In every pot to wipe out poverty?

Or would you just change
Your weekly numbers
To make sure you won
The lottery?

What would you change
If you could change?

To Whom It May Concern

I didn't even
Know her name,
But I was attracted to her
Like a moth
To an open flame.

The sweet smell of her perfume
Made my head dance
Whenever she entered a room.

Thou shall not lust.
Thou shall not lust.
Oh, how I used to have
Sinful, wicked dreams
Of the two of us –
Enough to make
The devil proud.

But she doesn't
Even know my name.
To her, I'm just another
Face in the crowd.

What Is My Charisma?

Is it my chocolate-coated skin?
Is it the way I commit
My sin?

Is it the way, each night,
I seem to break you in?

Or is it the freaky tales
That you love to tell
Your friends?

Girl, tell me,
What is my charisma?

Light

Light, light.
How you are so bright.

I turn you on
When I have a fright.

Oh, light, you are
All my might.

Jasmine
Nicole
Florio
"06"

Beauty Like Yours
Never Seems to Fade

Even though you've
Seen hard times,
Your face never seems
To show an age-line.

When I look at you,
I often wonder
How could it be
That a woman could possess
Such natural beauty.

You're always smiling,
And your face
Just seems to glow.

The beauty that you have
Inside of you,
I bet a lot of women
Would like to know.

But what they don't understand
Is that it's neither woman
Nor man-made,
But rather, simply,
Beauty like yours never
Seems to fade.

53

Mistake

A mistake isn't
A mistake if you
Didn't learn from it.

And if you repeat it again,
Then you're definitely hard-headed.

So you'll have to find out what?

That old saying that goes
A hard head makes for a soft butt.

Blessed child

Oh, what a blessed child
I am
To be the son
Of the Father of man.

For a while, darkness
Was all that I saw,
'Cause at first,
My eyes were closed.

But now that they're open,
All I see are
Beautiful rainbows.

And now I have
A better understanding
Of what's going on.
At times when I am weak,
I call upon His name,
And I'm made strong.

Dummy

Illiteracy is my tale,
Because I heard the truth,
But refused the sale.

I didn't want to be
Held accountable for my actions,
So I decided to just
Let it go.

Every time somebody asked
Me why,
I just dummied up
And said I don't know,
Thinking that was enough
To get me by,
When deep down inside,
I knew that was a lie.

I played the role of a *dummy*,
'Cause I was scared
To learn something new.

Po Folks

Every day It's a new reason.
It's a new season.

I'm on trial for my life,
Convicted of treason,
'Cause I don't subscribe
To what they believe in.

But if you're seeing
What I'm seeing,
Then you know
We should question
The so-called "people
Who make the rules",
'Cause they're playing us for fools.

We need to have a march,
Take it back, do it old-school
Like Malcolm and Martin,
Get it started,
Have a new world party.

They're lying to my face,
Having some debate,
Trying to figure out
Some other man's fate.

But they're fake like snakes,
'Cause their prize is the cake.

Crooked politicians, another Watergate.
So get locked and loaded,
'Cause wise words have been quoted.

We have a face.
We have a voice.
We are much more
Than Po Folks.

Conversation

I couldn't love you,
'Cause you don't love yourself.
I couldn't help you,
'Cause you wouldn't help
Yourself.
How you expect me to
Do for you
What you wouldn't
Do for you?
In order for you to
Get a real man,
You got to be a
Real Woman.

I'm just keeping it real,
Telling you the truth.
Good loving
Is only good for the night.
It ain't paying the water,
Gas or light.
I'm just saying
You got to be able
To put a little something
On the table.
Don't hate me, baby.
This is just good, old conversation.

Black Love

From city to city,
To state to state,
It's all the same.

I got nothing but love for you.
I don't need to know your name.

They say the world is a ghetto.
Well, if the truth be told,
Then the whole world is my area code.

It excites me to see people who
Look just like me wherever I go.
'Cause it remind me that
Black is beautiful.

Brothers, love your sisters.
And sisters, love your brothers.

Black love;
That's what I'm speaking of.
We started civilization.
It all started with us.
So let's act like true kings and queens
and step up.

God's Hands

It was God's hands that gently shook me
This morning and said it's time to get up.

It was God's hands that saved me
From my jump,
When I no longer cared and wanted to give up.

It was God's hands that fed me
and protected me
Throughout the years.

It was God's hands that dried my eyes and
wiped away
All my tears.

It was God's hands that pointed me in
The direction that I needed to go.

It was God's hands
That led me to the river, washed away all my
sins and cleansed my soul.
It was God's Hands!!

I Miss You

You may be gone, but you're not forgotten.
I remember the talks we used to have.
I hear them quite often.
I used to wonder why you had to be the
first to go.

But now I see you're spreading your love,
Just like a rainbow.

I hope you're smiling,
Looking down on me,
Seeing the man that I've come to be.

I can't wait to see you one last time.
I miss you.
You'll always be alive in my heart
and in my mind.

Polar-Bear Cool

I'm cooler than a polar bear's toe nail.
Oh, well.
So when I die, you can send me straight to hell.
Condemned to hell,
I won't be afraid,
Just as long as I can bring a tall glass
Of lemonade.

I'll let the ice cubes cool off my tongue –
Might even be tempted
To give the devil some
And set up stands and lemonade shops.
Might even get rich if I sell bomb pops.

'Cause I'm cooler than a polar bear's toenail.
Oh, well.

Knowledge

She saw me walking down the street.
She ran up to me,
And this is what she said.
She said, "Oh, Mr. Chocolate,
You're so sexy."
I said, "Sure you're right. God don't make no
mistakes."
She said, "You believe in God?"
I said, "For me, that's a no-brainer.
Every time I look at my three kids,
I'm reminded of God's little angels."
She said, "I like the words that you speak."
I said, "I'm a poet. I can talk about more than
what's happening in between the sheets."

For me,
I like to leave you
With something that's educational,
Spiritual and uplifting –
The tools you can use to defeat
The ignorance, 'cause
We're all victims; that way we can make
The world a better place to live.
If I'm a teacher, it's my responsibility
To give knowledge.

To Be or Not To Be?

To be or not to be?
That is the question.
But what is the answer?

Will I or won't I
Be one of life's famous little dancers
And leave my footprints tracked in the snow
So the world can take notice and say,
"A star is born.
There he goes; there he goes"?

My God

My God is a caring and loving God.

My God is a God most high.

My God is the Alpha and Omega,

The beginning and the end.

My God is a God who can remove all sins.

My God is a jealous God.

You shall have no other god before Him.

Fear

Fear is a cancer that can eat away at your dreams.

Let's not forget the saying: *Things are never as bad as they might seem,*

and remember to realize the only way to

defeat fear is with a win.

Pure

I am pure in my heart and in my mind
though my body has sinned time after time.

That's really on such a small scale
for natural acts like that
am I condemned to hell?

Cause as a man thinks then so is he.

I think purity and that's what keeps me free.

And my actions are further proof
that I'm a man who possesses truth.

Cause the truth is our cure.

That's why I am a man who's pure.

My Love

My Love
is so erotic and exotic
it's hypnotic

That even when you're awake
you'll still be daydreaming
about it

Good vibrations
see I bring this

I'm making love to you with my mind
as well as my penis

Stroking you mentally
as well as physically
getting deeper than deep

Now I know your
feeling me

Listen

Listen to a man's heart
when he has nothing to say

Cause sometimes words
can get in the way

Listen to the sounds of a teardrop streak
as it runs down his cheek

Cause sometimes a man
will let his emotions speak

For those who have ears
let them hear

Listen

What I Need

I need a friend lover
and confidant

I need someone
to be all that I am not

I need someone to be
the air that I breathe
to live

I need someone to be
my partner
my true Adams rib

If

If I never meet you
would I still dream about you

If I never see your face
would I ever know the
beauty about you

If I never felt your touch
would I ever know my heart
was capable of beating so much

If you ever left me
would I simply fade to dust

Wise Saying

True friendship is judged

By the miles,

Not by the smiles.

Do you agree or disagree with this proverb?

Think of ways you can apply this proverb to your daily life.

Wise Saying

A smile is free,

But can be worth

Millions.

Do you agree or disagree with this proverb?

Think of ways you can apply this proverb to your daily life.

Wise Saying

Poverty is

A great motivator.

Do you agree or disagree with this proverb?

Think of ways you can apply this proverb to your daily life.

Wise Saying

A promise is nothing

But words that we

Intend to keep.

Do you agree or disagree with this proverb?

Think of ways you can apply this proverb to your daily life.

Wise Saying

Whatever you want,

Name it,

Claim it

And Frame it.

Do you agree or disagree with this proverb?

Think of ways you can apply this proverb to your daily life.

ജ∞ജ∞ജ∞ജ∞ജ∞

Wise Saying

Prayer is your

Life force.

Do you agree or disagree with this proverb?

Think of ways you can apply this proverb to your daily life.

ഉ൭കഉ൭കഉ൭കഉ൭കഉ൭ക

Wise Saying

Understand while you're

Waiting for your turn,

Your turn may never come.

So sometimes in life,

You got to make

It your turn.

Do you agree or disagree with this proverb?

Think of ways you can apply this proverb to your daily life.

Wise saying

War is a crime

Against humanity.

Do you agree or disagree with this proverb?

Think of ways you can apply this proverb to your daily life.

ഊൈഊൈഊൈഊൈഊൈ

Wise Saying

Remember, even

The mighty elephant

Fears the mouse.

Do you agree or disagree with this proverb?

Think of ways you can apply this proverb to your daily life.

ഊൈഊൈഊൈഊൈഊൈ

Wise Saying

Remember, your

Thought pattern

Can be your blueprint

To success.

Do you agree or disagree with this proverb?

Think of ways you can apply this proverb to your daily life.

Wise Saying

Love is the four-

Letter word

Opposite of hate.

Do you agree or disagree with this proverb?

Think of ways you can apply this proverb to your daily life.

Wise Saying

Dare to be great.

Do you agree or disagree with this proverb?

Think of ways you can apply this proverb to your daily life.

Wise Saying

The wise, old owl

Became so smart,

Because he enjoyed

The silence.

Do you agree or disagree with this proverb?

Think of ways you can apply this proverb to your daily life.

Wise Saying

If fish is brain food,

Then God is soul food.

Do you agree or disagree with this proverb?

Think of ways you can apply this proverb to your daily life.

❦❧❦❧❦❧❦❧❦❧

Wise Saying

The reflection of your

Mirror is how the world

Views you.

Do you agree or disagree with this proverb?

Think of ways you can apply this proverb to your daily life.

❦❧❦❧❦❧❦❧❦❧

Wise Saying

Be slow to anger,

But quick to laugh.

Do you agree or disagree with this proverb?

Think of ways you can apply this proverb to your daily life.

Wise Saying

The discipline of

Collecting pennies can

Lead to great wealth.

Do you agree or disagree with this proverb?

Think of ways you can apply this proverb to your daily life.

Wise Saying

A dream is a reminder

Of things to come.

Do you agree or disagree with this proverb?

Think of ways you can apply this proverb to your daily life.

Wise Saying

In the event that

Tomorrow never comes,

What did you accomplish

Today?

Do you agree or disagree with this proverb?

Think of ways you can apply this proverb to your daily life.

ಶ)ಜ಼ಶ)ಜ಼ಶ)ಜ಼ಶ)ಜ಼ಶ)ಜ಼

Wise Saying

Your voice is a great

Instrument; use it.

Do you agree or disagree with this proverb?

Think of ways you can apply this proverb to your daily life.

Wise Saying

Bathing removes the

Outer dirt.

Prayer removes the

Inner dirt.

Do you agree or disagree with this proverb?

Think of ways you can apply this proverb to your daily life.

Wise Saying

Those who wait

Are often last.

Do you agree or disagree with this proverb?

Think of ways you can apply this proverb to your daily life.

ഇൟരുഇൟരുഇൟരുഇൟരു

Wise Saying

The truth is warm

And comforting like

A blanket.

Do you agree or disagree with this proverb?

Think of ways you can apply this proverb to your daily life.

ഇൟരുഇൟരുഇൟരുഇൟരു

Wise Saying

If kindness is a gift,

Make every day Christmas.

Do you agree or disagree with this proverb?

Think of ways you can apply this proverb to your daily life.

Wise Saying

Two wrongs

Don't equal a right,

But one right can

Equal the wrongs

Of long ago.

Do you agree or disagree with this proverb?

Think of ways you can apply this proverb to your daily life.

Wise Saying

Consider a bruise

Part of the learning

Experience.

Do you agree or disagree with this proverb?

Think of ways you can apply this proverb to your daily life.

Wise Saying

Never sell yourself short.

Always go long.

Do you agree or disagree with this proverb?

Think of ways you can apply this proverb to your daily life.

ʒ๛ଓ๛ʒ๛ଓ๛ʒ๛ଓ๛ʒ๛ଓ๛

ᏚᎾᏣᎬᎾᏣᎬᎾᏣᎬᎾᏣᎬᎾᏣᎬ

Wise Saying

Invest in love.

The returns are

Wonderful.

Do you agree or disagree with this proverb?

Think of ways you can apply this proverb to your daily life.

ᏚᎾᏣᎬᎾᏣᎬᎾᏣᎬᎾᏣᎬᎾᏣ

᠊ᠣᠣᠣᠣᠣᠣᠣᠣᠣᠣ

Wise saying

We are all

Fathered by the One.

Do you agree or disagree with this proverb?

Think of ways you can apply this proverb to your daily life.

᠊ᠣᠣᠣᠣᠣᠣᠣᠣᠣᠣ

Wise Saying

If you choose

To be a fool,

Then you'd better

Learn to duck.

Do you agree or disagree with this proverb?

Think of ways you can apply this proverb to your daily life.

Wise Saying

A dollar can never

Replace the words

"I love you".

Do you agree or disagree with this proverb?

Think of ways you can apply this proverb to your daily life.

Wise Saying

Only you can kill

Your dreams.

Do you agree or disagree with this proverb?

Think of ways you can apply this proverb to your daily life.

Wise Saying

Love is a recipe

That the world

Should share.

Do you agree or disagree with this proverb?

Think of ways you can apply this proverb to your daily life.

Wise Saying

Children are God's

Little kisses.

Do you agree or disagree with this proverb?

Think of ways you can apply this proverb to your daily life.

ഇൗരുഇൗരുഇൗരുഇൗരുഇൗരു

Wise Saying

Goals are the

Stairway to success.

Do you agree or disagree with this proverb?

Think of ways you can apply this proverb to your daily life.

ഇൗരുഇൗരുഇൗരുഇൗരുഇൗരു

Wise Saying

Jesus listens

When no one else

Listens.

Do you agree or disagree with this proverb?

Think of ways you can apply this proverb to your daily life.

ΣΟCRΣΟCRΣΟCRΣΟCRΣΟCR

Wise Saying

An excuse is never

A reason for failure.

Do you agree or disagree with this proverb?

Think of ways you can apply this proverb to your daily life.

ΣΟCRΣΟCRΣΟCRΣΟCRΣΟCR

Wise Saying

When you feel

You have nothing else

To give,

Give a piece of your

Heart.

Do you agree or disagree with this proverb?

Think of ways you can apply this proverb to your daily life.

Wise Saying

Learn how to pray,

Then pray often.

Do you agree or disagree with this proverb?

Think of ways you can apply this proverb to your daily life.

Wise Saying

Ice cream

Is a rainbow

For your tongue.

Do you agree or disagree with this proverb?

Think of ways you can apply this proverb to your daily life.

ಬಿಂಬಿಂಬಿಂಬಿಂಬಿ

Wise Saying

God doesn't make mistakes; we do.

Do you agree or disagree with this proverb?

Think of ways you can apply this proverb to your daily life.

ಬಿಂಬಿಂಬಿಂಬಿಂಬಿ

Wise Saying

A smile is the best medicine on the market.

Do you agree or disagree with this proverb?

Think of ways you can apply this proverb to your daily life.

Wise Saying

God's open 24 hours.

Do you agree or disagree with this proverb?

Think of ways you can apply this proverb to your daily life.

ରେକ୍ରେ

Wise saying

Wise men study every day.

Do you agree or disagree with this proverb?

Think of ways you can apply this proverb to your daily life.

ରେକ୍ରେ

Wise Saying

Jesus is the roadmap leading to the stairwell of Heaven.

Do you agree or disagree with this proverb?

Think of ways you can apply this proverb to your daily life.

Wise Saying

We all have birthmarks, but what is the mark you'll leave on the world?

Do you agree or disagree with this proverb?

Think of ways you can apply this proverb to your daily life.

Wise Saying

There are 24 hours in a day.
Choose one and make a difference.

Do you agree or disagree with this proverb?

Think of ways you can apply this proverb to your daily life.

Wise Saying

To keep a secret you must first shut your mouth.

Do you agree or disagree with this proverb?

Think of ways you can apply this proverb to your daily life.

✦∞✦∞✦∞✦∞✦∞

Wise Saying

A man's heart is his biggest muscle of all.

Do you agree or disagree with this proverb?

Think of ways you can apply this proverb to your daily life.

✦∞✦∞✦∞✦∞✦∞

Wise Saying

Love is like good coffee.
It must be brewed daily.

Do you agree or disagree with this proverb?

Think of ways you can apply this proverb to
your daily life.

Wise Saying

To live your life for yourself is selfish.
That is why it is called mankind.

Do you agree or disagree with this proverb?

Think of ways you can apply this proverb to your daily life.

Coming Soon!

SEX JUNKIE IS A VERY INTIMATE, PERSONAL AND OFTEN HILARIOUS LOOK INTO THE LIFE OF ONE OF KANSAS CITY'S MOST ELEIGIBLE BACHELORS, DAMON WILLIAMS. IF YOU'VE ONLY HEARD OF A SEX JUNKIE AND NEVER ACTUALLY MET ONE, THEN THIS IS THE PERFECT BOOK FOR YOU. LIKE A HIGH DEFINITION T.V., DAMON BRINGS YOU UP-CLOSE AND PERSONAL INTO HIS WORLD OF NON-STOP SEX. AND, LIKE A PLAY-BY-PLAY COMMENTATOR, DAMON GIVES YOU THE REAL LOW DOWN ON SOME OF HIS TORRID SEXUAL CONQUESTS. SO, GRAB SOMETHING COOL TO DRINK, 'CAUSE THIS READING MATERIAL IS DEFINITELY HOT!!!

---AND, LADIES, DON'T WORRY, THE NAMES HAVE BEEN CHANGED TO PROTECT THE GUILTY...

Coming Soon!

Triflin

RAYMOND FLORIO

TRIFLIN IS A PERFECT EXAMPLE OF WHAT CAN HAPPEN WHEN A "DEAR JOHN" LETTER TURNS DEADLY. DAMON HAS TO LEARN THERE ARE THREE THINGS THAT YOU DON'T DO TO A MAN: YOU DON'T MESS WITH A MAN'S FAMILY, A MAN'S MONEY, AND YOU DEFINITELY DON'T MESS WITH A MAN'S WOMAN. DAMON HAS TO LEARN THESE LESSONS AND LEARN THEM HE SHALL.

Coming Soon!

Wild BOYZ

RAYMOND FLORIO

EVER WONDER WHAT IT'S LIKE TO LIVE LIFE ON THE WILDSIDE? WILD PARTIES AND WILD WOMEN, WELL READ AND LEARN ABOUT THE DAY TO DAY ACTIVITIES OF DAMON AND HIS TWO HOME BOYS, JAX AND TY. DURING THE DAY THESE ARE THREE HIGHLY RESPECTED BLACK BUSINESS MEN IN THE COMMUNITY. BUT YOU KNOW THE SAYING, "THE FREAKS COME OUT AT NIGHT?" WELL THERE'S ANOTHER SAYING YOU SHOULD KNOW TOO... "HELL HATH NO FURY LIKE THAT OF A SCORN WOMAN!"